ILLUSTRATOR'S
REFERENCE
MANUAL
SPORT

ILLUSTRATOR'S
REFERENCE
MANUAL
SPORT

BLOOMSBURY

A QUARTO BOOK

Copyright © 1992 Quarto Publishing plc

Published 1992 by
Bloomsbury Publishing Ltd.,
2 Soho Square,
London W1V 5DE.

ISBN 0-7475-1305-8

This book was designed and produced by
Quarto Publishing plc,
The Old Brewery, 6 Blundell Street,
London N7 9BH

Senior Editor: Honor Head
Art Editor: Penny Dawes
Design: Elly King

Art Director: Moira Clinch
Publishing Director: Janet Slingsby

Typeset by QV Typesetting, London

Manufactured in Hong Kong by Regent Publishing Services
Limited
Printed by Lee Fung Asco Printers Limited

All pictures supplied by Sporting Pictures, UK Ltd. Special thanks
to Steve Brown for his help in the selection of the pictures used.

This manual has been compiled for artists and illustrators as a
guide to different sports positions and movements. To ensure
accuracy and authenticity photographs of professional sports
people have been used. However, model release has not been
obtained from the individual sports personalities for promotional,
advertising or commercial purposes and direct reproduction or
representation of the personalities featured within this book is
prohibited. For permission to use any of these personalities for
the above purposes, please contact their accredited
representatives.

The CIP record for this book is available from the British Library.

Contents

The ILLUSTRATOR'S REFERENCE MANUAL: SPORT comprises over 80 sports divided into the following categories — Ball Sports, Athletics, Gymnastics, Combat Sports, Weightlifting, Target Sports, Water Sports, Winter Sports, Adventure Sports, Cycle Sports and Horse Sports. Each category is numbered and within these categories each individual sport has its own sub-number for ease of reference.

Within each individual sport, design permitting and as appropriate, the main poses are divided as follows: singles/solo then doubles/group shots; male then female shots are followed by mixed where applicable. Where possible, poses of the same nature, ie bowling, goal scoring, serving, have been grouped together, but look through all the pictures given for a sport before making a final choice.

Single figures from a number of different sports or the same sport can be grouped together to form a composite picture or, in many instances, a single figure can be extracted from a group shot. The pictures have been chosen to ensure maximum scope and flexibility for the artist.

Pose title

Category heading

Code number

Subcode number

ATHLETICS: MALE

Running · relay · hurdles

2.01

ILLUSTRATOR'S REFERENCE MANUAL: SPORTS

USA

CITY OF CARDIFF

BIRMINGHAM

IMPORTANT

PLEASE NOTE: All the pictures used in this book are of sports professionals to ensure the body positions are accurate. The pictures are provided for this purpose only —they are not provided as models for exact and recognizable depiction and the publishers cannot accept responsibility for any such use.

Tennis – male singles

Tennis – male singles

Tennis – male singles

Tennis – male singles

Tennis – male singles

Tennis – female singles

Tennis – female singles

Tennis – female singles

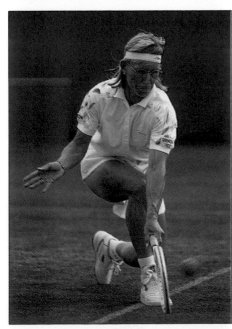

Tennis – female singles

Tennis – female singles

Tennis – doubles

Tennis – ball girls and boys · court officials

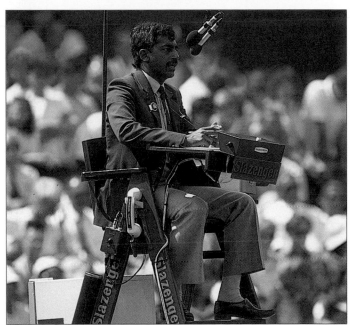

Table tennis – male

Table tennis – male/female

Squash

Badminton – male singles

Badminton – female singles · doubles

1.08   **Baseball**

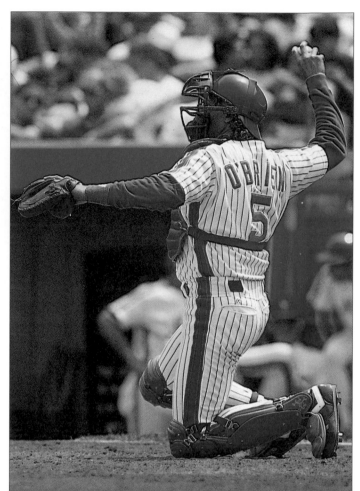

Baseball

Baseball

Softball

Croquet

1.11

Lacrosse

Lacrosse

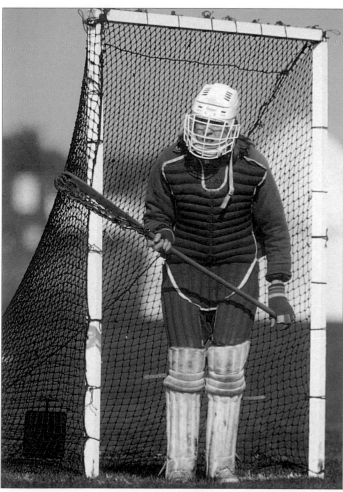

1.12

Cricket – male

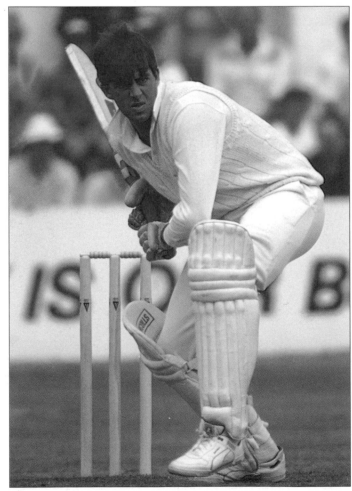

Cricket – male

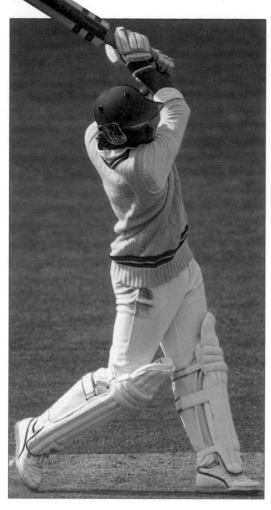

Cricket – male

Cricket – male

Cricket – male

Cricket – male

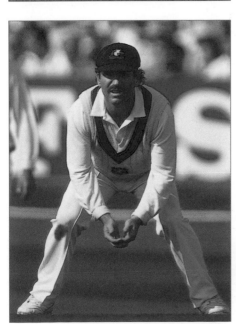

Cricket – male

Cricket – female

Golf – male

Golf – male

1.14

Golf - male

Golf – male

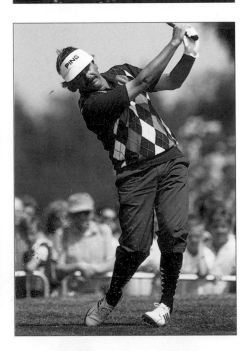

Golf – female

Golf – female · caddy

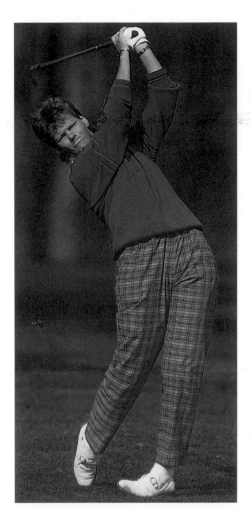

Hockey - male

Hockey – female

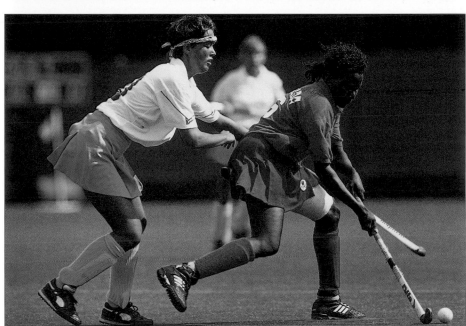

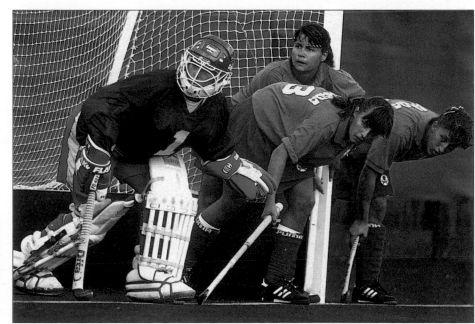

1.17 Basketball

Volleyball – male

Volleyball – female

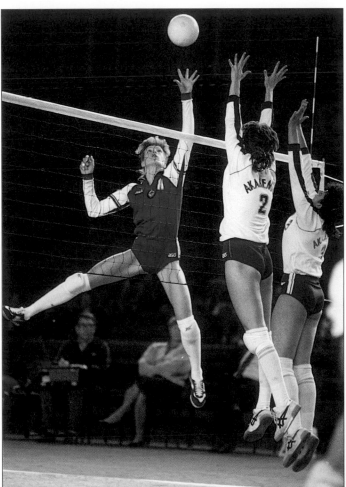

1.19

Football

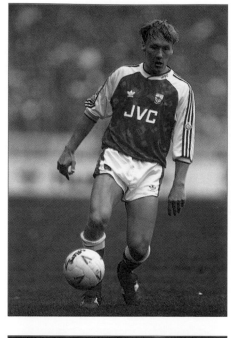

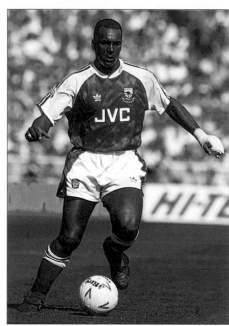

Football

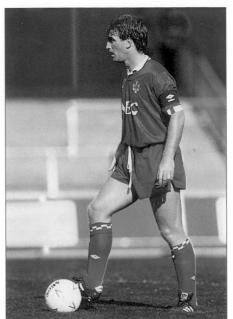

Football

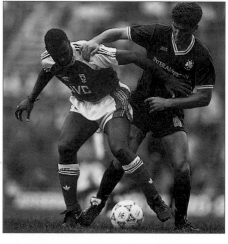

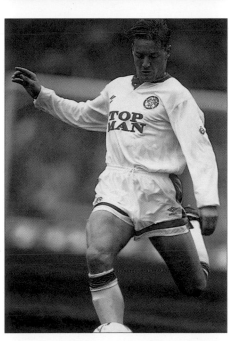

Football

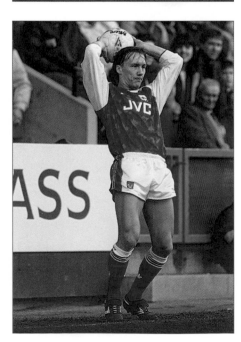

Football

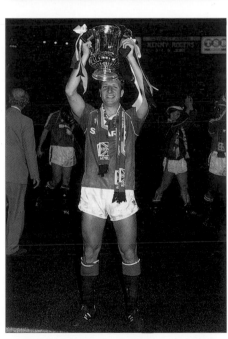

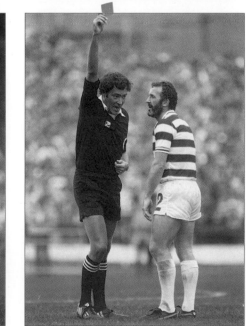

American football

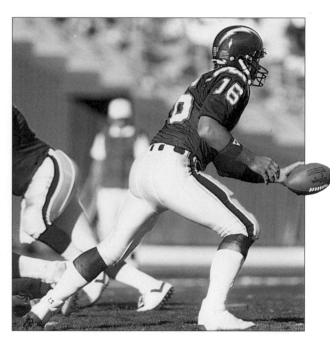

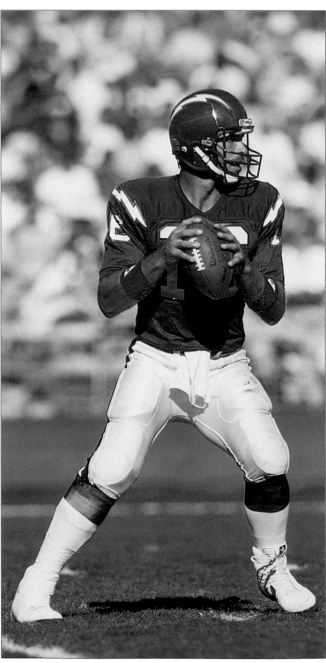

American football

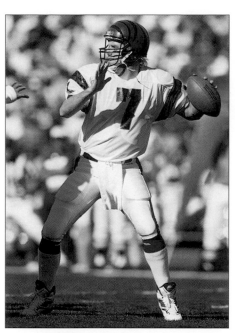

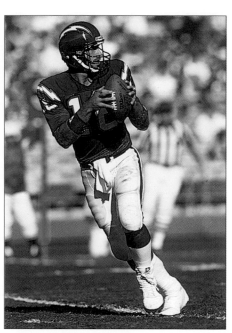

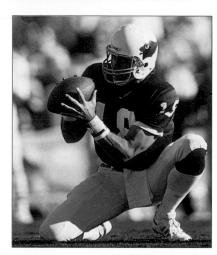

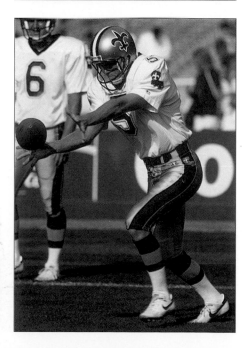

American football

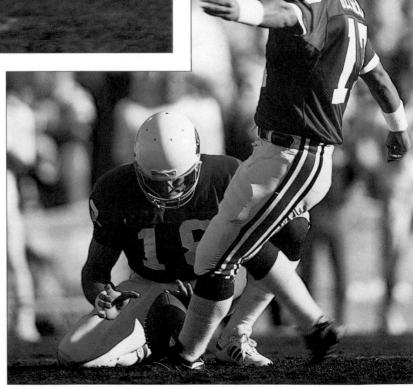

American football

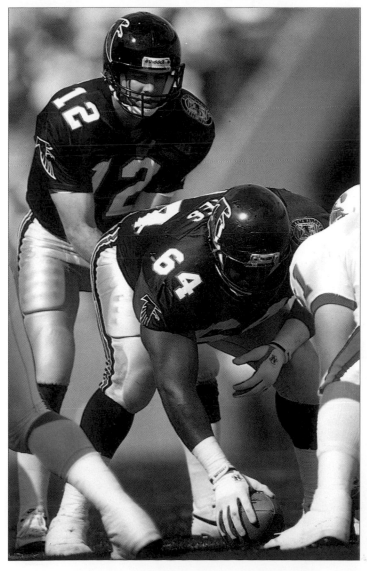

American football

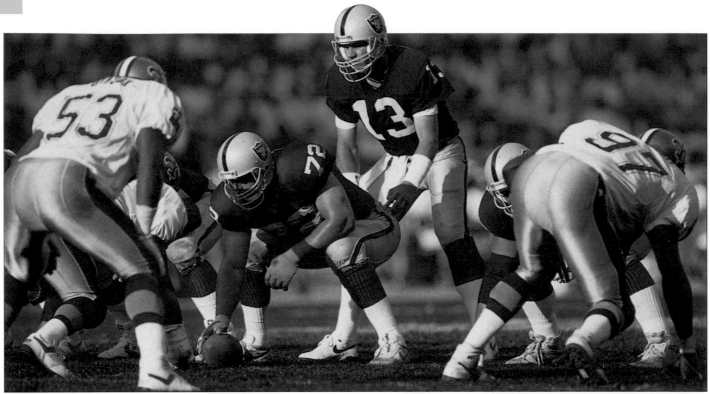

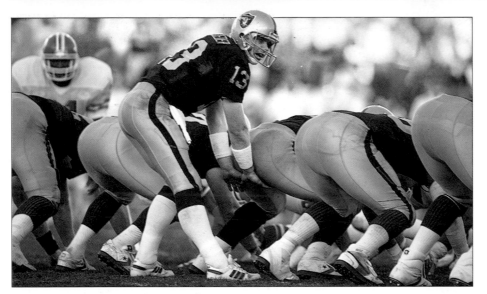

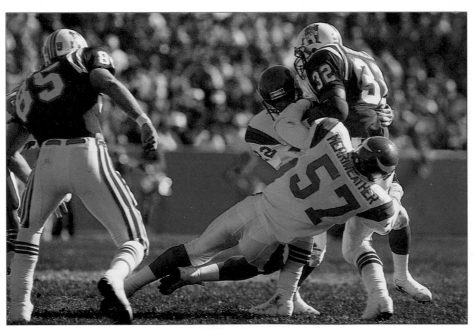

Cheerleaders

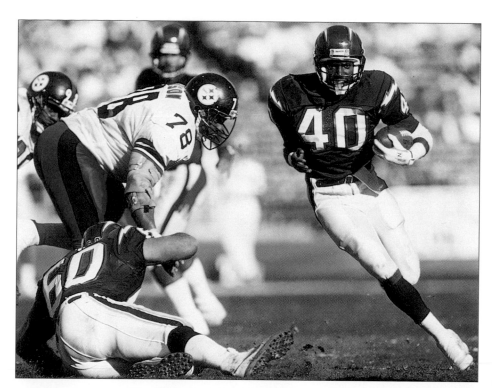

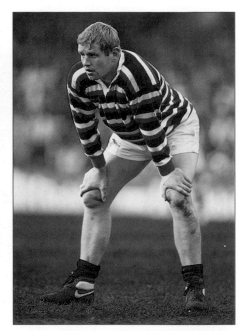

1.21

Rugby Union

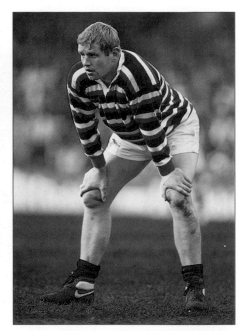

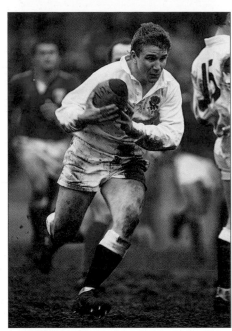

Rugby Union

Rugby Union

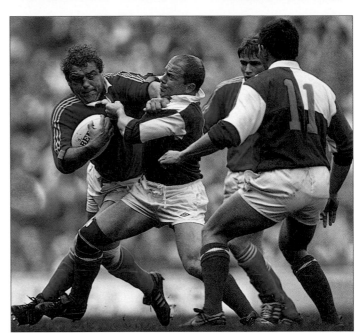

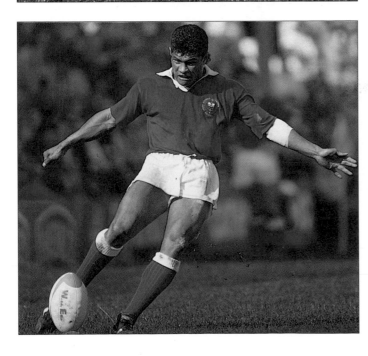

Rugby Union

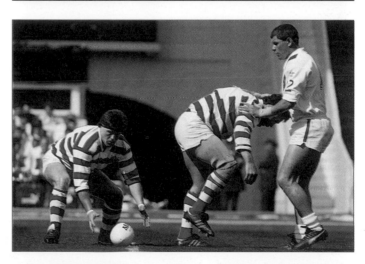

Rugby League

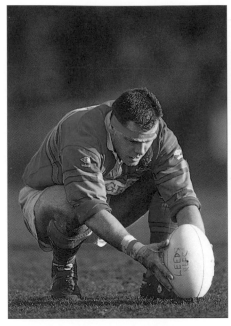

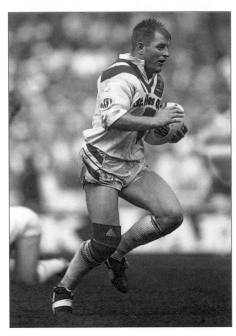

Rugby League

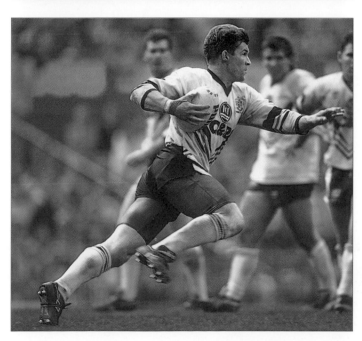

Bowls

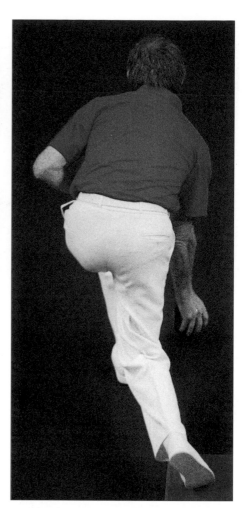

Snooker – male

Snooker – female

2.01 Running – starting

Running

Running

Running – relay · hurdles

Running – hurdles · steeplechase

Running – finishing

Running – marathon · cross country · speed walking

Long jump

2.02 High jump

Pole vault

2.03

The javelin

The discus · the shot put

Hammer throwing · track officials

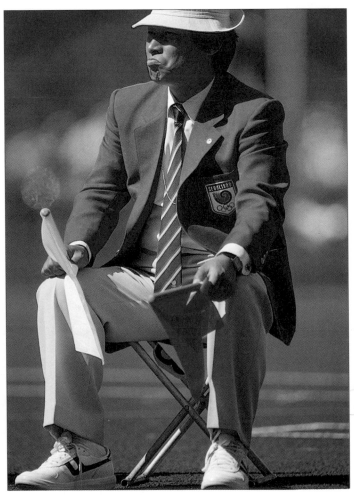

Long jump

High jump

The javelin

Horse

Rings

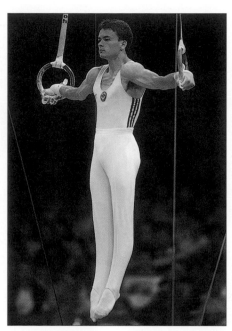

Parallel bars

Floor exercises

Asymmetric bars

Beam

Floor exercises

Floor exercises

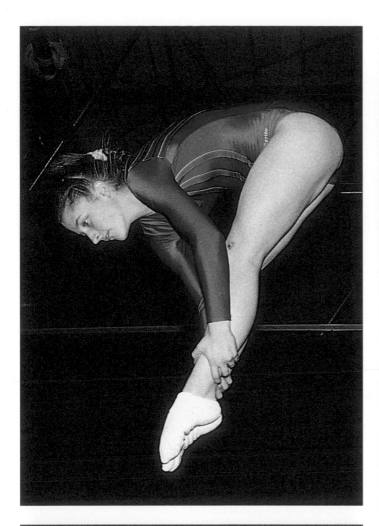

Fencing – male

Judo

6.04 Wrestling

Sumo and arm wrestling

6.06 Boxing

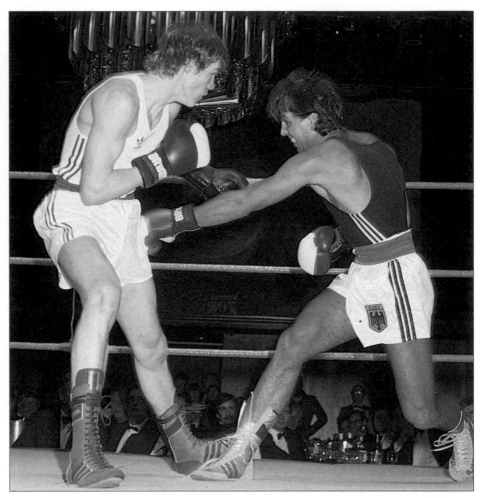

Shooting - skeet

Shooting – clay pigeon

8.01

Shooting – pheasant · small bore rifle

Shooting – small bore rifle

8.02 **Archery**

Archery

9.01

Diving - male

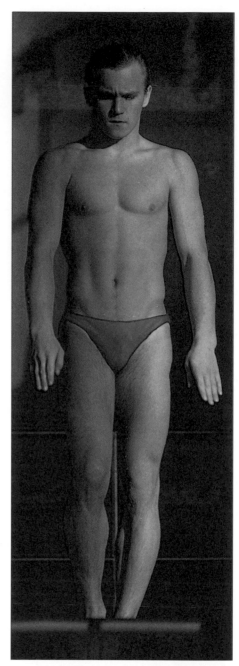

Diving – female

9.02

Swimming – male

Swimming – female

9.03

Synchronized swimming

Synchronized swimming

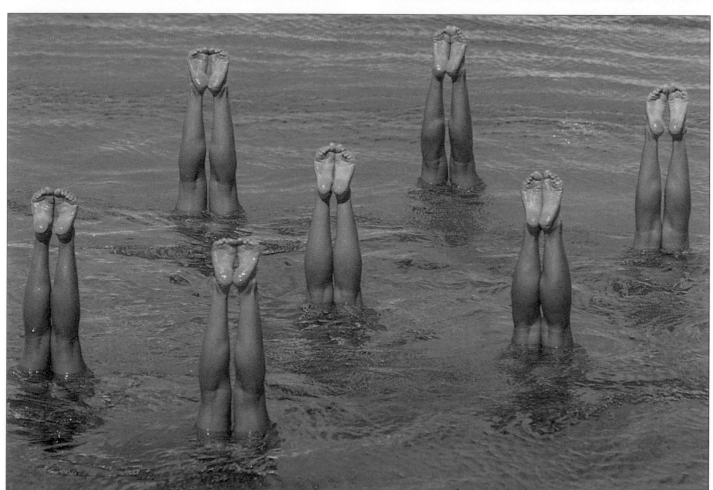

Surfing

Windsurfing

Windsurfing

9.06

Water skiing – male

Water skiing – female

Canoeing

Rowing – male

Rowing – male/female

9.09

Sailing

9.10 Fishing — fresh water

Fishing — fresh water

Fishing — fresh water

Fishing — sea

Skiing — male · downhill · slalom · cross country

Skiing – male · cross country · biathlon

Skiing – male · ski-jumping

Skiing — female · downhill · slalom · cross country

10.02

Snowboarding

Bobsleigh

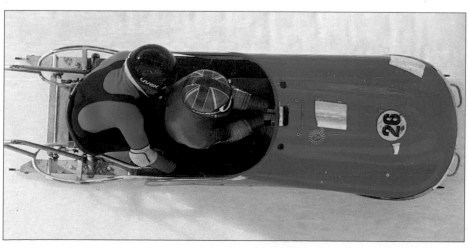

10.04

Luge · tobogganing

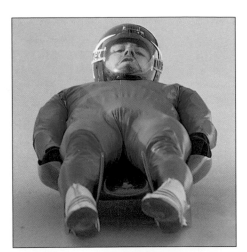

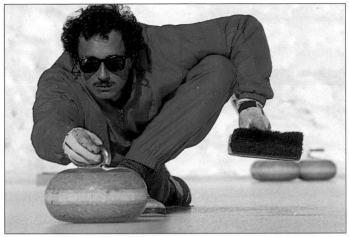

Skating – male · speed · figure

Skating – female

Skating – female

10.08

Skating — pairs · dance

10.09

Ice hockey

11.01

Rock climbing – male

Rock climbing – male/female

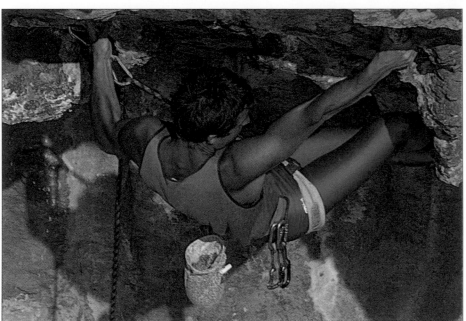

11.02 Hang gliding

12.01

Cycling – BMX · cross country

Cycling — track · road

Dressage

Flat racing · hurdles

13.02

Horse racing – hurdles

Cross country

Show jumping

Show jumping

Carriage driving

Carriage driving

Carriage driving

13.06 Polo

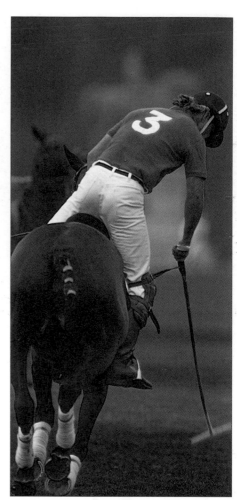